Organize your Life, Create Peace of Mind

By: Jasmine Alexander

Table of Contents

Introduction

Get Peace of Mind through Organization – Is it possible? How many times have we told ourselves that we need to manage our important information and organize it?

Every time you look for something, misplace something, fill out a form, the message keeps popping up like a reminder that simply won't go away.

Then, one day it's staring you in your face and you can no longer ignore it!

I was awakened by my personal experiences, which led me to the realization that organizing one's life is an essential part of living.

In this book, I am going to share with you how to clear your mind, how to take the paper clutter out of your life and put it into a tool or template that keeps you organized and readily available at your fingertips. My name is Jasmine Alexander, and I know firsthand what it's like to be faced with a situation where you need information, but you don't have it available when you need it the most.

Several years ago, I got a call from the hospital that my mother was in the emergency room. When I arrived at the hospital, the doctors and hospital staff had a number of questions regarding my mother's health history, allergies, medications, insurance and her advance directives.

Unfortunately, I didn't have any of that information. I felt inadequate and unprepared to help her.

I wondered how many families actually have their information organized and are prepared for such emergencies. Do they know what information is important to gather, sort and organize? Or, how long to keep important documents?

I have a background in technology. I had helped develop many online products. I figured there was such a software solution for managing one's information. I began to look for solutions to track family information.

I ran product development and technology departments for companies including content management, website, analytics and operations - everything that goes along with running high traffic websites.

I knew how to develop software systems both from experience and education. I have worked for several large companies as their Chief Information Officer. Companies like Penton, Ziff Davis and ABC.

I have bachelor's degree in Computer Science and a Master's in Business Administration from UCLA.

Based on my research, I was shocked to learn that there just weren't any effective ways to have the papers and the information we need in our day to day life available in an organized, searchable and electronic form.

To further complicate matters, most people simply don't know what information is important or how long it needs to be kept. There is a lot of confusion about legal terminology and Internal Revenue Service guidelines, financial and other regulations. These need to be sifted through to get a clear idea of what needs to be kept, maintained and updated regularly.

The Discovery Process

According to surveys, we spend an average of 6 weeks looking for things. Whether in an emergency or over the course of daily life… that is a lot of time!

If you are in an emergency, you are already in a stressful situation where you need to make a lot of decisions. Ideally, this is not the time to be looking for vital information.

If you have your information gathered, sorted and organized, you can access it whenever you need to. Even simple things like filling out a job application or renting a car can be extremely time consuming when you can't easily access the information that you need.

I was looking for a software solution that would make these everyday needs easier. I wanted more than a storage system like Google drive, Evernote, or

Dropbox. These are great tools to store information, but you have to create your own techniques to use them effectively. These solutions are definitely better than nothing.

But, I wanted more than a storage solution.

The functionality of the software that I was looking for needed to provide alerts, search, sharing, dashboards, analytics, and most of all, easy access.

When I found no practical solution, I took on the mission of creating a software solution that is helpful for day to day life, changes in family situations, accommodates regulatory, legal and financial changes, and estate planning.

After months of development, the software is now up and running and my family has all of our information organized and is easily accessible at Jazmine.com.

Breakthrough

I started by interviewing my circle of friends, family and people about how they managed their information. It turned out that most families don't have their information organized or they have parts of their information organized and in many cases only one spouse knew where the information was.

I also realized that most people didn't know what information was important to keep or how long to keep it and how often it needs to be updated.

I started by creating intake forms, typically used by financial and estate planners. I turned these into spreadsheets.

Originally, I captured information on a spreadsheet. I found out very quickly that spreadsheets are just not robust enough to handle every family scenario and are difficult to keep updated.

I then created a database and this became the basis for my new software.

And then that was it. I knew I had to create something robust and dynamic.

Essentially, I knew that I had to commit to building software.

I also realized that I needed to provide education. I would hear comments like: "I don't need a will because I don't have enough." Or "If I plan ahead, I might die sooner." Or, "If I set up a trust, I will lose control." And so on…

Capabilities

Our lives are becoming more and more digital with each passing day. As technology becomes pervasive in our lives, we create more and more information about ourselves, our homes and assets. It is now more important than ever to gather, sort and organize this information.

How would a person managing your affairs for you handle things like your eBay, Amazon or Netflix accounts or a popular blog or an online business that could still be financially viable when you are ill, or even beyond your life? How do they keep it running? How do they fill orders for existing customers, continue to create new content, or continue marketing products? Will they have a way to access the sites and/or the information that it takes to run that business?

People often say, "I don't know that I have enough stuff," and yet I think if you really looked around in your life, when you go through your wallet or when you go through an inventory of all the items in your house, all your medical information, you will begin to see just how much stuff you have. No matter what financial level you are at there is paperwork. Then, as your income grows, the financial information, the paperwork that is created through those finances grows as well. New accounts and information need to be tracked and organized. As your life evolves, whether it's a marriage, move, job change, birth of a child or divorce, you continue to accumulate information.

Jazmine.com is a software solution that helps you organize and keep up with the information in your life. It gives you access to information anytime you need it.

You can selectively share all of your data or selected categories with trusted family members and advisors. You can change this at any time.

You can upload documents related to a particular item whether it is a scan or a copy of the original document and indicate where the original is stored.

You can search by keywords or look for a contact, such as an accountant.

The software will automatically alert you if something is about to expire or if it has already expired.

It aims to be your virtual assistant for your family information!

The Twelve Categories of Life Information

According to my research, most individuals have twelve categories in their life.

They are:
1. Personal Information (Wallet items)
2. Legal Documents
3. Health (Medical, Dental, Vision, Other)
4. Finances
5. Insurance
6. Real Estate (home)
7. Vehicles
8. Pets
9. Collections
10. Storage
11. Digital
12. Miscellaneous or Custom

There are also several life events that create more information or changes in information, such as:

- Marriage
- Birth of a child
- Admission or Graduation from School/College
- Job Changes
- Moves
- Divorce
- Death in family

Many of these events happen many times during one's life. A person in this generation has an average of 8 jobs during his/her career. Imagine the amount of information that generates!

Each category and life event has been thoroughly researched for the type of information that needs to be tracked, including regulatory requirements, or information needed by other software that you or your advisors may use.

For example, in the Real Estate section, you can input information about your property, including the contents of your home and maintenance schedules. You can save home improvement information so that you have that available for taxes or when you sell your home. You can save photos of inventory items by room and you can save information about major home appliances such as the hot water heater, furnace, elevator and so on. If major maintenance needs to be done on an item, you can create a follow-up date which will send you an alert when that item is due for service.

As another example, the Pets category allows a pet owner to input their pet's medical information from their vaccination certificates, info about groomers, walkers, boarding centers, clothing, food, animal hospital, veterinary information and notes in an organized way.

Once you get this done, you will achieve Peace of Mind.

When Life Gets in the Way

During my research and subsequently working with my own family and clients, I discovered that most people prioritize the urgent and not the important.

The time that you set aside to get the important stuff sidelined, because there is no milk, or there is a leak or a problem of some sort. It doesn't get rescheduled and ends up on the ever growing list of things to be done someday – until of course, that someday becomes today!

Unfortunately, when it finally gets on the urgent list, it is because some other emergency caused it to get there. Usually, this will cause additional stress on an already stressful situation.

Being proactive by setting aside a few hours every month or year can save you countless hours of lost productivity and potentially save you lots of money.

All of us have getting our information organized on our list of things to do.

We just have to get started. The good news is once you decide to get started, I can show you how to keep going and what information needs to be gathered, sorted and organized so you can feel guilt-free and achieve peace of mind.

Overwhelmed!

By the time we are in our 40's or 50's, we have accumulated a significant amount of information. If you are just starting to get organized you may be so overwhelmed that you simply want the whole problem to go away!

I understand! I have seen this happen to many of my clients.

Burying your head in the sand and procrastinating or any other avoidance method will not simply make the problem go away. In fact, it will make it worse because you will continue to generate more information.

If you need help, you can recruit your siblings or children. They can help you gather the old stuff, take old books to the dump, shred, gather, sort, organize and so on. Or, you can hire a professional organizer or administrator.

Ideally, a professional organizer or admin will also set up a paperless system and enter the information so that you and your family can access it at any time and keep it updated.

Having your information organized can help you when it comes time to file your taxes, take the proper deductions when you buy or sell your home and save you money because your accountant or estate planner isn't starting from scratch.

Also note that much of the information in your wallet, your credit card account information, travel documents, birth and marriage certificates and other important information is usually not tracked by an advisor. An estate planner does not have their client's driver's license or passport information. However, this information can be easily tracked within the software. The software will also alert you before items expire.

Not Just For The Wealthy

Wealthy people keep more of their wealth! Why? Wealthy people know that if they don't plan ahead, create the right documents and setup the proper financial instruments such as trusts and insurance policies, most of their wealth will end up going towards taxes and not to their loved ones. First, they have advisors and experts to tell them what is wise to do. Second, they can afford to pay for advisors.

They know that taxes are the biggest drain on inheritance during their lifetime and after. In order to reduce their tax burden and maximize their family's inheritance, they have their information and plans in order. Wealthy people aren't emotionally attached to planning. They know that planning is important and that it needs to be done.

Unfortunately, most people are misinformed, both about the things that they can do to manage their stuff as well as the fact that they should be managing it. Whatever you don't focus on and whatever you don't manage, will become an unwieldy beast. It doesn't have to be that way!

I have heard people say countless times: "I don't have enough to be bothered with getting my stuff together."

"It's too expensive." You have heard the saying "It takes money to make money." Hiring an expert can cost money, but, in most cases, they save us a lot of money. They have spent years training and working with many clients and can do the same for you.

The fact is every state in the United States has probate laws. These were created so that your estate can be administered by the courts if you didn't provide a Last Will and Testament. If this is the case, a probate judge will determine the fate of your family's inheritance (after taxes of course).

Planning can only be done while you are alive and able.

There are indeed some simple things you can do now that will help you during your life and, your family, after you have transitioned.

1) Your state's Living Will documents can be downloaded free, executed by you and shared with those closest to you and your medical advisors. These sets of documents are commonly called "Advanced Directives". In some states, you can also file these with the Attorney General's office for a small fee.

2) Sign a HIPPA release form and file it with your doctor and those closest to you.

3) Create a Last Will and Testament. Handwritten wills are no longer valid in many states.

4) Organize your information and share with your executor, family or advisors as you wish.

You can find links in the resources section.

If this is not something you want to do yourself, you can hire an estate planning attorney. You can find one in your area by searching for one at the National Estate Planning Council's website (see link in resources).

Estate planners are attorneys with many years of training and can structure your estate for maximum tax benefit and risk mitigation. They typically charge hourly or may have a package for creating a simple estate plan. However, they need most of your information in order to create a plan. If you gather, sort and organize your information, they won't need to charge you for this, which is the first step in the estate planning process.

Get Educated

As your income and family grows, it falls to you or your partner to educate yourselves about how to manage and organize your information and plan for the future.

Unfortunately, this is not taught in colleges and universities. We learn these important skills through trial and error, or worse, when confronted with an emergency.

To further complicate matters, the legal and financial terminology is confounding at best, and legal experts differ on what is important and how to do things.

While I was researching features for the software, I read many books, articles, spoke with experts and potential clients about what to do, what was important to know and keep and how to go about creating a family database or binder.

I created a series of articles and webinars to help you learn and serve your family the best way possible.

You don't need to become an attorney or financial planner, but, knowing some basics will help you ask the right questions and find the right experts.

The Emerging Affluent

As your income grows, you might be in the category of people that financial institutions call "Emerging Affluent". These are families with annual household income of $ 100,000 or more and $500,000 to $5 million in investable assets.

You may be an entrepreneur, a small business owner or an employee climbing the corporate ladder.

As the emergent affluent grow their income, assets and families, it is extremely important to keep track of each family member's personal information. Each member may have several jobs through their careers which means multiple stock option plans, 401k or similar plans, pension or other retirement plans and so on. It is simpler to start getting stuff organized before it becomes something necessitated by a major crisis.

A Message to Women

During my research, I discovered that a majority of women actually rely on their spouses to organize and plan their estates. They find out later that things haven't been planned properly, or inadequate insurance policies exist or even simple things such as beneficiaries have not been updated.

Women live on average 5.6 years longer than men. Therefore, it is very likely that the male spouse will pass away before the female. I have heard many stories where women found out that their plans were inadequate to support their future. It is definitely a double whammy when you are dealing with grief and loss on top of trying to figure out how to pay for your loved one's funeral, pay bills and access accounts.

Ideally, you know where your checking account is, insurance policies and other important information, so you can attend to your grief and your family in stressful situations.

Planning is easier and better done when we have our cognitive capabilities. In other words, not after the onset of Alzheimer's or Dementia. We are better able to articulate what our wishes are, who inherits what and so on when we are lucid. We can be proactive now so that our family members aren't left dealing with the crisis and stress of taking care of us.

We NEED to know where our information is.

Where do I Start?

I created the 5 STEP system to help you get started with minimal preparation and anxiety. You can get set up and then go through one category a week if that works for you. If you follow this method, it will take you about 13 weeks or 3 months. Imagine that in 13 weeks you can get your paper clutter under control, know where everything is and achieve Peace of Mind!

The 5 STEP Process to Peace of Mind

1) Set up for success
   - Set aside regular time
   - Get a shredder if you have a lot of stuff to get rid of or call a shredding company to haul away your stuff and shred it for you
   - Get a label maker and labels
   - Get a Scanner or Smartphone app for scanning
   - Folders for filing originals
   - Download Paper Retention Schedule to select records to keep

2) Select, shred and sort
   - Proceed in this order:
     - Garage and Attic
     - Home Office
     - Kitchen
     - Other rooms where there is paper

- Sort into Categories by family member
  - Keep each family member's stuff together
  - For example, don't put all passports in one file

3) Missing/Follow up
   Set up two baskets
   1) Missing items
      a. If you find there are items missing as you go through your category sweep, take a piece of paper and write down what is missing. Put it in the box or basket. When you have time go through each and do what is necessary to get the information. For example, you may have to download a form from the DMV for a duplicate title and send it in with a

check. Once you have done this, move this piece of paper, with a date of when you sent it in and copies of what you mailed to the waiting for basket.

2) Waiting for

Once you have received what you have been waiting for, file and update it in the right section.

4) Category sweep

- Proceed in this order for each family member. If you have preferences, change the order, but, make sure you go through every category.
  - Wallet
  - Health (Medical, Dental, Vision)
  - Real Estate
  - Vehicles

- Financial
- Legal
- Pets
- Collections
- Digital
- Other

5) Maintenance/Update

Review once a month, quarterly and annually. Update your statements, passwords, check your beneficiaries and other information as necessary.

Conclusion

I am passionate about helping you organize your information. I will continue improving the software and create resources that are helpful for you.

I have shared quite a bit of information with you here. You can get further information on specific topics at jazmine.com.

I invite you to get started today!

Resources

For articles and software:
https://jazmine.leadpages.com/organize
-your-life-ebook

Paper Retention Schedule:
https://jazmine.leadpages.co/paper-
retention-schedule/

Advance Directives for your State:
http://www.caringinfo.org/

National Estate Planning Council:
www.naepc.org

Legal Documents:
www.legalzoom.com
www.nolo.com
www.rocketlawyer.com

HIPPA Release Form:
http://www.cumc.columbia.edu/hippa/d
ocs/litigation_auth_English.pdf

Disclaimer:

The information contained in this ebook is for general information purposes and while I have made every attempt to keep the information up to date, I make no representations of warranties of any kind, express or implied, about the completeness, accuracy, reliability, suitability or availability with respect to the website or the information, products, services or related graphics, photos contained herein or any references.

The references provided have their own terms and conditions on their website and you are subject to their terms and conditions.

In no event, shall we be liable for loss or damage including without limitation, indirect or consequential loss or damage, or any loss or damage whatsoever arising from loss of data or profits, or in connection with, the use of this ebook and resources.